Kahlil Gibran
The Beauty of Friendship

Kahlil Gibran

The Beauty of Friendship

Illustrated by
Donni Giambroni

HALLMARK EDITIONS

8 - 87

Edited by Kitty McDonald Clevenger.

Text reprinted by arrangement with The Citadel Press and Philosophical
Library, Inc. from *A Treasury of Kahlil Gibran*. Copyright 1951 by The Citadel
Press. *A Second Treasury of Kahlil Gibran*. Copyright © 1962 by The Citadel
Press. *A Third Treasury of Kahlil Gibran*. Copyright © 1975, 1973, 1966,
1965 by Philosophical Library, Inc. *Spiritual Sayings of Kahlil Gibran*.
Copyright © 1962 by Anthony R. Ferris.

We live upon one another according
to the law, ancient and timeless.
Let us live thus in loving-kindness.

We are friends.

I want nothing from you,
and you want nothing from me.
We share life.

To understand the heart
and mind of a person,
look not at what
he has already achieved,
but at what he aspires to do.

I love you, my brothers and sisters,
whoever you are.
You and I are all children of one faith,
for the diverse paths of religion
are fingers of the loving hand
of one Supreme Being,
a hand extended to all
offering completeness of spirit to all,
eager to receive all.

They say if one understands himself,
he understands all people.
But I say to you, when one loves people,
he learns something about himself.

The secret in singing
  is found between the vibration
    in the singer's voice
  and the throb
    in the hearer's heart.

Many a time I have made a comparison
between nobility of sacrifice
and happiness of rebellion
to find out which one
is nobler and more beautiful;
but until now I have distilled
only one truth out of the whole matter,
and this truth is sincerity,
which makes all our deeds
beautiful and honorable.

Love is the only flower
        that grows and blossoms
    without the aid of seasons.

Generosity is not in giving me
that which I need more than you do,
but it is in giving me
that which you need more than I do.

The chemist who can extract
from his heart's elements
compassion, respect, longing, patience,
regret, surprise and forgiveness
and compound them into one
can create that atom
which is called Love.

I saw Friendship strengthened
between man and all creatures,
and clans of birds and butterflies,
confident and secure,
winging toward the brooks.

The sympathy that touches
　　　the neighbour's heart
is more supreme
　　　than the hidden virtue
in the unseen corners
　　　of the convent.

You are here as my companion
along the path of life,
and my aid in understanding
the meaning of hidden Truth.
You are a human,
and, that fact sufficing,
I love you as a brother.

From a sensitive woman's heart
springs the happiness of mankind,
and from the kindness of her noble spirit
comes mankind's affection.

He who understands you
           is greater kin to you
than your own brother.
For even your own kindred
           may neither understand you
nor know your true worth.

Truth is like the stars;
it does not appear except
from behind obscurity of the night.
Truth is like all beautiful
things in the world;
it does not disclose its desirability except
to those who first feel the influence
of falsehood.

The heart's affections are divided
like the branches of the cedar tree;
   if the tree loses one strong branch,
       it will suffer but it does not die.
   It will pour all its vitality
into the next branch so that it will grow
       and fill the empty place.

Of life's two chief prizes,
beauty and truth,
I found the first in a loving heart
and the second in a laborer's hand.

Your most radiant garment
  is of the other person's weaving;
Your most savory meal
  is that which you eat
    at the other person's table;
Your most comfortable bed
  is in the other person's house.
Now tell me, how can you separate yourself
  from the other person?

Humanity is a brilliant river
singing its way and carrying with it
the mountains' secrets
into the heart of the sea.

Truth is a deep kindness
that teaches us to be content
with our everyday life
and share with the people
the same happiness.

My brothers,

seek counsel of one another,

for therein lies the way out of error

and futile repentance.

The wisdom of the many

is your shield against tyranny.

For when we turn

to one another for counsel

we reduce the number of our enemies.

Love is the only freedom in the world
because it so elevates the spirit
that the laws of humanity
and the phenomena of nature
do not alter its course.

Tenderness and kindness are not signs
of weakness and despair,
but manifestations
of strength and resolution.

I have only human words
to interpret your dreams,
your desires, and your instructions.
But God has given to each of us
a spirit with wings,
Wings on which to soar
into the spacious firmament
of Love and Freedom.

You are my brothers and sisters
because you are human,
and we all are sons and daughters
of one Holy Spirit;
We are equal and made of the same earth.

Darkness may hide the trees
and the flowers from the eyes
but it cannot hide love
from the soul.

Your friend is your needs answered.
  He is your field which you sow with love
    and reap with thanksgiving.
… you come to him with your hunger,
    and you seek him for peace.
And let there be no purpose in friendship
    save the deepening of the spirit.

The flowers of the field
*   are the children of sun's affection*
*   and nature's love;*
*   and the children of men*
are the flowers of love and compassion.

I love you, my brother,
       wherever you are,
whether you kneel in your church,
    worship in your synagogue
      or pray in your mosque.

Knowledge and understanding
are life's faithful companions
who will never prove untrue to you.
For knowledge is your crown,
and understanding your staff;
and when they are with you,
you can possess no greater treasures.

The power to love
is God's greatest gift to man,
for it never will be taken from
the blessed one who loves.

Set in Bernhard Booklet designed by

Lucian Bernhard in 1935.

Book designed by Lavonia Harrison.